BIRTHWAY

BIRTHWAY

COLM CORLESS

Cló Iar-Chonnachta
Indreabhán
Conamara

First published 1995
© Cló Iar-Chonnachta 1995

ISBN 1 874700 04 4

Cover
Photograph by Thomas Quinn

Design
Cló Iar-Chonnachta

Cló Iar-Chonnachta receives financial assistance from the
Arts Council/An Comhairle Ealaíon

Publishers: Cló Iar-Chonnachta Teo., Indreabhán,
    Conamara. Fón: 091- 93307   Fax: 93362
Printing: Clódóirí Lurgan Teo., Indreabhán,
    Conamara. Fón: 091-93251/93157

For my parents

Acknowlegdments are due to *The Galway Advertiser* and *Criterion* in which some of these poems first appeared.

The poem *Flowers* was a prizewinner in the 1995 AIB/WESTERN PEOPLE BALLINA SALMON FESTIVAL and ARTS WEEK LITERARY AWARDS.

CONTENTS

A Farmers Prayer For Rain

The spuds are down for three weeks
and the cabbage in the two drills
by the wall
are down for two and a half.
My row of carrots are in
for a fortnight.
Its been the hottest driest season
since the weather can remember.

I stand by the garden wall
among my sunburnt drills,
the only moisture they've seen
are my sweat droplets.
I've stood on all points
of the cross,
praying for rain.

I Took a Drink, Lord

I took a drink, Lord,
from the cold steel waters
of the big bellied earth,
rose the cup
to my parched lumpy lips
and let its grip
run inside me
mudding the cracks,
drowning the itch of drought
at my mouth's roof
and swelling my sides.

I swelled my sides
on the earth's waters,
beyond Taibhreen, Niagara,
the tropics,
swelled like a bee's load of nectar.
And now I sit,
honeymaking.

BEALACH DAIGHIN

Bealach Daighin - a tight passage,
tight food and drink pipes
leading to the opening
of a stomach lake.

Bealach Daighin - a hilltop place name,
a place where drunkards
with their lips swelled
from night air and porter,
dismounted their black bikes.

Their big guts wobbled around here
in the dark hours of early morning;
they made sure they didn't fall
and break their teeth in their stupour.

These bachelor farmers
their stock and land drank,
with pinched holes in their livers
paused here nightly
as they tumbled abuse
on their gut-land.

PUT-DOWN DYLAN

That mongrel hound,
Dylan,
or had she good breeding?
She wouldn't chase a cow
or kill a rat,
but she followed the lethal injection
into the shed,
her tail wagging.

When the poison was delivered
her eyes looked at me
in full darkness,
before, as quick as a last heartbeat,
she lost all strength
and without twitching her tail
she died
between my father's hands
and my brother's.

THE PORTER DRINKERS

Between the ham slicer
and the fridge,
I saw them offer whiskey
to the heavens
while the porter drinkers cheered.

I leaned against the slicer,
and raised my glass each time
to calls for health and song.

They know how lost their prayers are
from previous blessings,
which did not hold off
liver and heart casualties
and lost parcels of land.

I left my emptied glass
on the slicer's ridge
and ordered more drink
as they laughed
in their smoky sanctum.

ROOFTOPS
for Aodh Ó Coileáin

Once, on a moonlit night,
by crevice and cleft,
I traversed the Galway rooftops.
I started in Mill Street
on a slippery mossy roof,
and by careful tact
I took my moon sodden way
to Nuns Island -
a high roof of clean slate.
From there, perilously,
and I won't tell you how,
I crossed the river
between the bend and bridge
and ended up in Bowling Green
where I sat on a chimney stack
and had a smoke
on a moonlit night
in Galway.

KNOTTING

In our hayfield
the baler wasn't knotting.
It's driver jumped down
from the bucking tractor
and manually tied one up.

He and my father
stood by the exit chute,
their sleeves rolled up.
They wiped the sweat
and hayseed from their foreheads,
and began tying twines.

My father's bales are produced
by a mechanical thing
if a fault happens,
he can be delayed a while
in a June meadow.

I too forage along perimeter rows
of harvest savings.
When my meticulous raking and saving
is not binding,
when the knot slips
and the maum lands in a jumble

on the cropped stubble of my field,
there are no manuals
in the sweat and dusty hayseed.

Instead, there is a displacement,
confusion and anger,
blunt blades of thought
and sun-glazed eyes.

I wrestle in the waves of heat,
with snapped wrapping
and blurring vision,
while my father follows
the baler across the meadows,
as it parcels neatly
his toasted brown rows.

WEB OF DREAMS

While I was lost
in a web of sleep,
some old dream hero
searched for his princess
across the caves
of the world's seasides,
borrowing a ship's sails for wings.

She waits undiscovered
with a bunch of flowers
by a stream.

I was disturbed
by a bottle breaking on the street;
my dream people became frozen
to that smash on concrete.

Can I wind on manually
in my conscious torque
the film strip of dream?
Will they loose their flowers
amongst the mayflies?
Will she find another man?
Will the ancient hero
become jaded and fail?

My conscious hours
are a dilemma –
spin me another web of dreams.

BACHELOR

A bachelor put his heels
in the driveway gravel
as the dust cleared.
Dogs barked,
a flock of birds rose,
flapping and startled,
into the sky,
The children ran into each other,
delerious, and gabbling his name.
He was such a rare sight
in the house.

'Two bullocks' he said
from the back door jamb,
head poking in sideways
hands spread in his pockets,
the dogs snuffing at his leg.
Quickly silent,
the children watched
their parent's attention.
All eyes,
bright wide blinking lamps;
trying to remember seeing
two lost bullocks.

'I saw steaming dung
in the lane' the father said
with all authority;
The runaways were in
the long laneway to the old school.

The bachelor went on to talk
on dogs, low walls, hot weather;
he did not come in past the back door,
and grunted at the suspicious dogs as he left.

Life returned to normal,
the bachelor passing without stopping,
raising dust clouds with his car,
on his solitary way
around his empty acres.

BANKING POEM

Last week,
you won't believe it,
I went into the bank
for more money.
The Teller's eyes
nearly popped clean out of his head,
another thousand!
His ears twitched a lot
he dropped his biro,
walked up and down
pretenting to be searching for bits of paper;
he even forgot how to add
as he asked me about my father's farm,
Berlin, Canada,
and the farming life in general.
Then, after waiting to let
the enormity of the situation
dawn on me completely,
he begrudgingly handed me over the smackers.
I tell you
I couldn't drink it fast enough.

Bob

Bob regularly wandered out
on the monochrome moonlit land
his tail held a whoosh behind him
in search of, I don't know,
doggie things.

Even if he saw anything worth mentioning
he wouldn't carry it home to us,
he'd just be there on the doorstep
in the morning,
as we stepped over him to school,
gold and white blaze of his pus
left on his paws,
with perhaps a briar caught in his tail.

He'd howl at the moon
making our hair stand on end,
then he'd stake his claim
from under his hind leg,
scuffling with female guests
on Corn Sack Boulevard
behind the barn door.

While our heads rested
behind moonlit walls,
old Bob was master
of fluttering ceremonies.

BIRTHWAY

The cow we hunted
from the Summer's field,
her birth bag slapping
the cheeks of her arse.
In the crush,
my father's hand and arm,
lubricated by washing up liquid,
investigated inner wombs,
the cow heaving frightened breath
through her nose,
while I held the tail.
'We'll need help' he said
as his withdrawing arm
gurgled out of the troubled birthway.

With two others to help,
my father found the crubeens
and slid a knot to the knuckle
on the backwards bearing calf.
Backed now from the crush,
we laid our weight
in birthing rhythm,
two to a side,
on the ropes.
Thighs appeared,

tail next
and with an easy sigh
the calf slid out from the dews sack
and thumped on the concrete.

Hands sought out her mouth
to release a birth breath.
She heaved a strangled call
and stilled.
Her mother,
oozing with blood,
sniffed with a flicking tongue,
then straightened her back
away from her ejected property.

We slid it into the transport box,
wordless,
reversed to the bushes dump,
jerked the release mechanism,
and it fell
between the blooming white thorns
to the bottom rocks.

At our washbasin
we washed cowshite
and birth blood from our hands.
When the taps stopped
there was a numb silence
in the world.

FLOWERS

I picked wild flowers,
fuschia, hedge, carnations,
sprigs of holly,
and made them into a bunch,
and walked up the river path
to see Suzanne,
beyond the tree avenue
where the bugs frizzled
under the lamplight.
With my prayer ready
and my heart on my ears' anvil,
I pressed the doorbell,
but nobody stirred within.

The flowers dropped to my side,
my grip weakened
out along the path
where later her feet would come.
Dropped the pink,
the orange, the fuzzy green.
She might observe
a causeway of colour there
and scent on the wind
the crimson smell
of their crush.

A Ballad To Be Read In The Dark

Of all the darkest things to be written
let me go further
and write only what is to be read
in the dark,
the central paradox being
that by the very fact that it is dark
this poem can't be read
and can only be heard
from memory, or tape,
in the dark.
So it is doomed from the start
this little giving from me,
because this metal clip in my heart
has sprung and is inflexible to all,
a ballad to be read in the dark
that will never be read in the dark.

Next time I'll use a flexible title
and a workable feeling
and I won't throw the oars away
before I've cast off
from my watermark.
(It sort of leaves you hanging, I suppose).

LAST STAND

I felt a pressure in my head
this morning,
but I paid it no mind.
I needed my pension in town
so I jumped on my bike,
turned past the cross roads,
and on to the village.

I was aware
of people looking at me
after I got my pension,
Someone was calling
for a doctor
and a glass of water.
I've done alright for seventy five years
I told them as I left the shop.

It must have been
up around the supermarket
that the power went in my legs
and I sank like a car in water.

There was a hissing in my head
as I remembered that me
and my now gone on cousin Liam
bridled a horse at this spot
years since.

A girl with white socks
was looking at me,
and I glimpsed
the collar of a priest,
as blobs of darkness appeared.

I was slipping further
when I felt a warm hand
and a jab on my arm.
Next I was lifted to a car.

I noticed the jackdaws
picking among the shorestones
with the little starlings
by the pier
as I was driven out the County Road.

HONEYPOT

I have a pot
of Nora Connolly's honey
in my hand,
and I won't let it fall,
like I did with the workmen's tray
of cups and saucers.
Nora is so proud of her bees,
I'm delighted for her pots,
its better than scraping it
from the timber combs
and sucking the wax from your teeth.

Nobody saw me go
with the big spoon from the drawer,
down Balla Glas bothareen
to eat myself into a sticky mess.

I lie in the grass
and take the elastic cover off,
dip and twist the spoon
and stick it in my gob,
licking the spoon clean.

Two ladybirds crawl up my arm
and a wasp butts the jar,
but I'm half way down,
my head cradled
in the crook of my elbow
among the foxgloves.

Nobody will find me here
until I'm left with a knob of honey
that I won't want to eat,
and I hear them calling
across the fields
my lost syrup-coated name.

BUSH CUTTING

I took the file from its paper,
and, bracing the hook
between the steering arm of the tractor
and the front axle,
with one way methodical strokes,
I brought a tender edge
to the ash-handled tool,
and leaning it on my shoulder
went to the far field
and set to the west wall
not hacking,
but slicing at the root.

Uncovered,
the blackthorn, blackberry,
briar and fern,
beheld mossy,
sometimes brown,
gentle green headlands,
which I rolled aside
beside the vertical bumps of limestone.

The briar
cutting with its downward thorns
my forehead,
my hands rightly torn,
now and again using my saw,
the blackthorn though tough
yielded under my edge
and left a fresh perimeter
on my acres.

BRÁISTEACH

A Summer's day when I was a teenager,
my father brought me weeding
our three acre potato garden.
I stood still at the drill tops,
unwondering at the symmetry,
and the green, brown and yellow;
it was the yellow we had to pull.

We set to it.
I counted the steps, bent over,
scrambling and grabbing at thistles,
so I could not think of my stalling heart
while thorns stung me to anger
as I tried to catch up with my father,
whose backside was bobbed upfield
rapidly widening the gap between us,
his hands tough from many stobs,
the thorns
and the weight of work to be done
bringing the tears.

Tears begone! I stumbled on,
standing on weeds in frustration
of hands and mind
that could not work fast enough,
and answer my desire to be finished.

A hundred yards further on,
over the hill,
in the first two drills beside the wall,
my father turned on the headland
having finished,
and came to meet me in mine.

The sun, our time-piece,
had moved from the east,
towards the south.

THE FIRST CUCKOO

Away over the acres
in old Jordan's wreck
I heard the first cuckoo croak.

Inventories of them
have visited first
that old ruin
where once old Jordan
broke incense
over a limestone bowl of dew
for the pecked traveller.

He calls softly every April
after the rains of Spring,
before he penetrates
the hot Summer hazes
and circles around,
robber for another's nest.

His grid is pinned
to Jordan's corner
where he bathes
with the graces
and pitches his voice
in the rain heavy land.

CLACKING

There came knocking
on my window
a lady with grainy eyes.
I let her into my white room
with red curtains.
She didn't stay long,
she just painted her lips
with a long pen,
rustled a few of my papers
and left;
she turned her nose
towards the suburbs.

I returned to my desk,
to write in slung phrases
sounds as elusive
and meaningless
as the clacking of her bike
on the paths.

GHOST

The house is deserted,
T.B. still hangs around
inside its cut stone walls,
the breeze sounds
through its surround
of sycamore and ash trees;
its cold keystone is broken.

A full family made it a warm home
out of the rough rocks around them,
and perished in it
before the thatch fell in.

Window openings still survive,
gaping roadward;
the sun and moon
through the swaying trees
make blinking shadows
across the empty rotting rooms.

MY VOICE IN THE WORLD

I will let my voice
break past the throat - lump,
this voice which, I was told,
was useless.

I will let these quivering vocals
burst down my nasal passage,
then I will hear and believe.

My voice will bounce new,
still smeared with birth blood,
and will rush quickly
past the ears of time.

It alone now
will fill a space
like my born dream
said it would.

My voice will echo
through my skull,
it will buzz in my ears,
I will utter these words,
tripping through them
like a boot top through grass.

Listen to it,
astounding me in its hum –
I am,
and here is my voice.

AFTERPOEM

I placed yellow bananas
on my desk,
took up a pen,
and waited to see
what would happen.

I shifted often
on my chair,
and scratched out
many times
all the things
I had written.

I decided to leave you
in the after-poem,
the area where
thought bugs flip and plummet;
remember the colour yellow
as I chew
on the subject of my poem.

WRITING POETRY

Writing poetry
behind the closed curtains of my room
at half ten in the morning.

I'd be in many other places.
if I wasnt rivited here
in a cradle of words.

I'm goo-gooing and kicking alone,
thumb-printing down lines,
dancing to airs, with graces,
practicing my waltz alone.